Mr. Mario's Neighborhood

Written by Galo Ramirez Illustrated by Bruce Martin

Hello, I'm Mr. Mario. Welcome to my neighborhood.
Let's go for a walk.

Today on our walk let's look for all the pushes and pulls that we can see.

Do you see a little girl pushing a fire truck?

4

How many other pushes and pulls can you see?

When this building is finished,
it will be our new library.
Do you see a worker pushing
a wheelbarrow?

How many other pushes and pulls can you find?

People come here to buy fresh vegetables and fruits. Do you see a father pushing a stroller?

How many other pushes and pulls can you see?

This is where the boats come after they've caught a load of fish. Can you see a worker pushing a cart full of fish?

How many other pushes and pulls can you see?

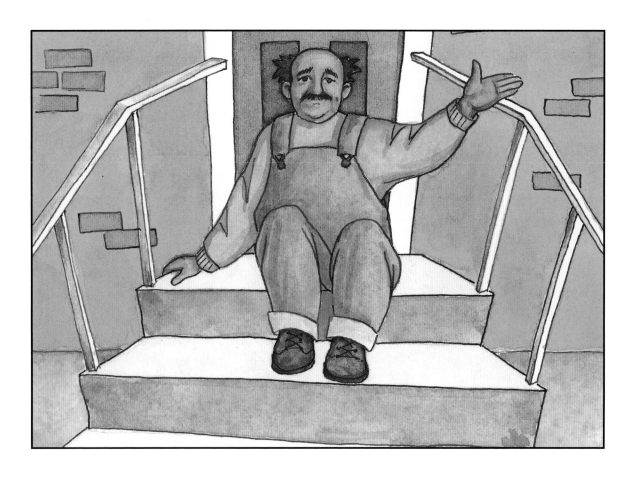

Pushes and pulls are everywhere. The next time that you go for a walk, see how many pushes and pulls you can find in your neighborhood.